John H. Dawson

CW00853269

PETER KRTEN

SERIAL KILLER

INTRODUCTION

Peter Kürten (born May 26 1883 in Mülheim am Rhein; died July 2 1931 in Cologne), called "The Vampire of Dusseldorf", was a German serial killer. The brutality of his murders and the hysteria that he triggered in the Rhineland made the search for him the most-noticed crime case in the Weimar Republic and also sparked international interest. The nickname that the press gave him at that time was due to an incident in December 1929, when Kürten killed a young swan in the Düsseldorf court garden and drank its blood. Police and court records show that he also drank or tried to drink from the blood of some of his victims.

YOUTH AND FIRST OFFENSES

Kürten was born on May 26, 1883 in Mülheim am Rhein, a then booming industrial city near Cologne. Here Kürten grew up as the third oldest of 13 siblings in modest living conditions. The father, a metal worker, was an alcoholic who beat his wife and children. At the age of five, Kürten, accompanied by a dog catcher, discovered his pleasure in killing while drowning two puppies in a stream. In his youth he injured numerous animals by stabbing them. After his father had once again assaulted his mother, Peter broke out at the age of eight. He lived on the streets for three weeks, supporting himself with minor thefts before he was found by the police and brought back to his parents. HIs mother prevented him from being subsequently admitted to a care facility.

Years later, after his final arrest, there was speculation as to whether Kürten was responsible for the youths that thad been found dead near the river at the time of his runaway episode, even though Kürten had been only nine years old. His guilt in those cases has never been established.

In 1894 the family moved to Düsseldorf. Peter attended elementary school in Gerresheim and then began a sand casting apprenticeship in the Düsseldorf factory, where his father was also employed. Corporal punishment of the apprentices was still the order of the day there. The father was sentenced to one year and three months' imprisonment in the same year for abusing his eldest daughter. That same year Peter choked a girl in the Grafenberg forest. A little later he embezzled wages and used the money to go to Koblenz and from there made a trip along the Rhine river with a prostitute. Back in Düsseldorf on June 6, 1899, he was sentenced for embezzlement to two months in prison, which he served until August 1899. Later, he was handed another two-day prison sentence for spending the night outdoors, considered as a charge of vagrancy under German law at the time.

After his release from prison, he stayed in Düsseldorf without a permanent job. He was now 16 years old and met the much older woman M., who also had a daughter who also had a daughter who was the same age as Kürten.He moved into their apartment, and engaged in violent sex with Ms. M. , including beating and choking her with her consent. After protests from house residents, the unequal couple separated. However, Kurten did not abandon Ms. M. and entered the apartment through a skylight to threaten her and rob her of her keys. For this he was sentenced to twelve days in prison on January

2, 1900. After he entered the woman's apartment again and threatened her, he was sentenced to another seven days in prison on February 16, 1900. Because of bilking, burglary and theft in 1900, he received three sentences. He then lived briefly with his mother, who had since separated from his violent father, but then he went to Rheydt, where he committed several thefts, for which he served time in prison in Derendorf until January 1903. At this point, it should have been obvious to anyone familiar with the young man that he was a serial offender, beyond rehabilitation through conventional means. But the authorities simply released him, and he was free to commit more, and ver more violent, crimes.

In the spring of 1903 he was living with his former classmate Elisabeth Brenner in Düsseldorf. After being expelled from the apartment by the Brenners, he terrorized the family by throwing windows in with rocks and an ax over several days, and firing several shots at father Brenner and the apartment. For this he was sentenced to a prison term of one year and three weeks shortly thereafter. After the term of imprisonment, he stayed with his mother, but was soon taken up again by Ms. M. He made his living by committing burglary and theft.

In the autumn of 1904, Kürten developed a great passion for arson, igniting haystacks and barns with matches and then watching the fire brigade's efforts to extinguish the fire. No suspicions arose at the

time of the fires. When he was later arrested on suspicion of murder, 24 arson attacks could be attrib-
uted to him, although the number of unreported
cases is probably much higher. Also in the autumn
of 1904 he was drafted into military service at the
98th Infantry Regiment in Metz , from where he
left on the first day to hide with Ms. M. again. After
his arrest on New Year's Eve in 1904, he was sentenced for desertion to seven years in, serious theft
in 34 cases and attempted theft in a further 12
cases. He served this sentence in Münster. He then
lived with his mother again, sometimes in a rented
room in Düsseldorf, and continued to make his living through burglaries.

Further offenses followed in rapid succession. A
maid with whom he had a relationship separated
from him for abuse. After molesting a woman in
a restaurant, he shot at guests rushing to help and
a security guard, for which he had to go to prison
again for six months. In a burglary on May 18, 1913
in Düsseldorf, he severely abused a 16-year-old girl
he came across in the house, but was able to escape
without being recognized.

FIRST MURDER AND SUBSEQUENT OFFENSES

On May 25, 1913, he committed the first clearly attributable to him murder. His victim was nine-year-old Christine Klein, whom he found sleeping late at night when he broke into the inn of an inn-keeper in Mülheim. He cut her throat and, without finding any valuables, escaped unnoticed. The victim's mother, who was still working in the inn on the ground floor, noticed the fact a few minutes later when she wanted to go to bed. Kurten returned to the crime scene the day after the crime, where he spent hours listening to the angry guests' conversations about what had happened. Fingerprints were not found at the scene, but Kürten had left a bloodstained handkerchief marked with his initials. Since the house owner and father of the girl, Peter Klein, had the same initials, he was initially suspected. After Peter Klein was able to prove his innocence, his brother Otto Klein - the victim's uncle - was suspected. He was incriminated by a witness who had seen a man in a suit like Otto Klein come out of the house. There was also an inheritance dispute in the Klein family, which served as a possible motive. There was a trial before a jury, but Otto Klein was acquitted due to lack of evidence. He fell during World War I in 1915 somewhere in Russia, without having been able to prove his innocence.

However, Peter Kürten was never suspected of having committed the crime.

In early summer 1913, Kürten had a short relationship with a domestic worker. At their second nightly rendezvous in the Grafenberg forest, he struck and choked her. Since dawn was coming and passers-by were nearby, he let go of her. At the subsequent breakfast together in a restaurant, the woman managed to escape, but did not file a complaint. Shortly thereafter, Kürten attacked a man with an ax in Gerresheimer Park, escaped undetected and, while still undetected, set fire to a straw-laden wagon while he was escaping. The following week he hit another girl in Gerresheim with the same hatchet and then set three haystacks on fire. A little later he attacked another girl with a hatchet when he broke into a house in Düsseldorf, but was then driven away by her father. He again managed to escape unrecognized.

On July 14, 1913, he was arrested, but nor for murder: he was sentenced to six years in prison for a string of thefts and burglaries. He served his term in Brieg; his sentence was extended another two years after he took part in a prison mutiny.

After his release in 1921, Kürten lived in Altenburg, where one of his married sisters lived. In Altenburg he worked in a machine factory, but also attracted attention through various animal cruelties. A violent assault on a girl he pushed into a ditch was not reported. In Altenburg he married Auguste Scharf in 1923. She had a criminal conviction for manslaughter with a firearm, and Peter Kürten was proud to have chosen her as a wife. In 1925, he and his wife moved back to Düsseldorf, where they initially lived at different addresses, before moving into a furnished apartment on Schwanenmarkt. Finally, they moved into an attic apartment at Mettmanner Strasse 71, which they lived in until Kürten was arrested. In Düsseldorf, Kürten was employed by construction companies and machine factories. His wife initially worked in a fish roasting kitchen, later in the kitchen of the Hemesath café on Graf-Adolf-Strasse, where she often worked late into the night.

For the neighbors Kürten was the loving husband, who often accompanied his wife to work with a well-groomed appearance and also picked her up again. No one suspected that Kürten could be a dangerous perpetrator of violence or that he wasn't exactly being faithful to his wife; in fact, he often raped his female acquaintances in the process of committing adultery. His wife knew of his infidelity because she had talked a few girls out of filing charges against Kürten. In the summer of 1925, he mistreated three maids in Düsseldorf's Parkstrasse at short intervals. The girls' trust was gained with fake papers in which he had made himself ten years younger and had a different occupation. One of the girls reported him for marriage swindling . The other two girls were also heard in the course of the trial, so that the violence also came to light. There was no conviction for rape, but Kürten had to serve a several-month prison sentence for falsifying documents .

In 1926 and 1927, Kürten committed a number of other attacks on women and arson, but remained undetected. In other cases he was sentenced to a total of eight months in prison for threats, insults and attempted coercion at the beginning of 1928, which he served in Düsseldorf-Derendorf until October 1928.

MURDER SERIES FROM 1929

Between February and November 1929, Kürten committed eight murders. Between February 1929 and his arrest in May 1930, he committed more than 20 break-ins, most of them with the intention of murder.

On February 2, 1929, he attacked Apollonia Kühn at 9 p.m. in Düsseldorf's Berthastraße and stabbed her several times with scissors. Believing he had killed the woman, he hid nearby. After the woman, who had been seriously injured, could still get to her nearby apartment, he returned briefly to the abandoned crime scene. A few days later, he returned to the scene of the crime and there involved a woman and her daughter in a conversation about the crime. He later had the scissors, the tip of which was broken off and stuck in the victim's head, regrinded. On this occasion, he also acquired a dagger. The mentally ill worker Johann Stausberg later falsely confessed to the crime, so that the case was considered solved. Only after Kurten's arrest could his guilt be established because of his confession and the evidence of the broken scissors tip matching the pair he still had in his possession.

In the evening of February 9, 1929, he went from Flingern to Gerresheim with a larger pair of scissors - so-called imperial scissors with embossed images of the imperial couple. Around 6 p.m. on Behrensstrasse, he met 9-year-old Rosa Ohlinger, who had got lost. He offered to take the child home and then took the direction to the address given by the child. At the Vinzenzkirche, just a few steps away from Kürten's apartment, he stabbed the child several times with the scissors he carried with him until she was dead. The crime scene was relatively invisible due to a construction site and was not illuminated in the evening. He then went to his apartment, cleaned the scissors and clothes and left the apartment to go to the Alhambra cinema, for which he had received a free ticket. After the movie screening, he returned to his apartment, filled a beer bottle with petroleum, and went back to the child's body. Since there were passers-by nearby, he could not set the body on fire, but he left the beer bottle at the scene of the crime. In the early morning of the next day, he returned to the scene of the crime, where the body had remained undetected. He poured petroleum on the body and set it on fire. He threw the bottle away, it was never found. Then he returned to his apartment. The body was discovered by construction workers early in the morning. The insane Stausberg later admitted this murder too. Kürten subsequently visited the crime scene several times. In the period that followed, he continued to use the construction site as a hiding place for his murder tools.

After the murder of Rosa Ohlinger, Kürten roamed the area of the attempted murder of Apollonia Kühn every day. He wore the same clothes as on the previous days and carried the scissors with him. However, he initially did not find a victim in a suitable place. On February 12, 1929, he was just about to return home when he came across the 54-year-old invalid Rudolf Scheer on the Hellweg near the allotment gardens of Gerresheim around midnight. Scheer had been drinking at a pub and was on the way to his allotment. Kürten stabbed him with the scissors and inflicted numerous wounds on the victim as he struggled. He also unsuccessfully tried to drink the escaping blood with his mouth. He then pushed the seriously injured Scheer down a bank where he died during the night. The body was found the next day by the same woman with whom Kürten had talked about the attempted murder of Ms. Kühn only a few days earlier.

In March 1929, Kürten met a single mother, whom he told that he was divorced. After closer questioning, he admitted that he had lied about his living conditions and attacked the woman.

In July 1929, Kürten was regularly out and about in the Zoo district , where he addressed women several times. Once, when he had already chosen a victim, he met his wife, who spoke to him ironically about his companion. Kürten, who had his scissors with him, left both women standing and ran away. Another time he persuaded a woman to visit the fair in Heerdt together. On the way back he choked her, but she managed to escape before he could use the scissors.

On August 8, 1929, he met the domestic worker Maria Hahn at Hansaplatz and agreed to go on an excursion with her for the coming Sunday. On that Sunday, August 11, 1929, they met again at Hansaplatz and took the tram and train to Neandertal, where they spent the day on a long hike. On the way back to Gerresheim, Kürten lured his victim with a trick onto a secluded meadow, where he choked Maria Hahn after initial tenderness and then stabbed her with the scissors he had brought with him. This time he drank the victim's blood, but soon vomited it up again. He put the body in a drainage ditch and then went home. His dirty and bloody clothes aroused his wife's suspicion, but Kürten had excuses ready. Nevertheless, he feared that he would be linked to the murder when it became known, so that the evening after the crime, he returned to the scene and first made sure that the body was still there. He then went back to his apartment to get a shovel, which he used to go to the crime scene again at night and to dig a grave nearby to hide the body. His wife hadn't missed the fact that he was out at night, but he could reassure her with excuses. In the period that followed, he frequently returned to the tomb - initially to disguise it better, and later to masturbate near it.

On August 20, 1929, Kürten went to the fair at Lierenfeld after work. He carried the recently acquired dagger with him and addressed several women without success. At around 2:00 a.m., he followed two girls on their way home to Gumbertstrasse 3, where one of the girls lived. After the first girl had arrived at her apartment, he followed the other girl, 18-year-old Anna Goldhausen, a few meters and stabbed her with the dagger in the upper body. However, the girl managed to escape, called for help and rang the doorbell at her friend's house at number 3, where they quickly opened, so that Kurten hurriedly fled. At around 2.15 a.m. he pressed a woman who went home alone, the 31-year-old Olga Mantel, who initially avoided him, but which he pursued and whom he stabbed several times in the back on Erkrather Strasse. Alarmed by the screams of the woman, a porter came over to the factory and chased the perpetrator but quickly lost sight of him. While fleeing, Kürten attacked another man, 30-year-old Heinrich Kornblum, with a stab in the back near the funfair square. Kornblum escaped and reached the fairground, where he received treatment for his wound. Kürten hid the dagger near Erkrather Strasse and hovered around the fairground for a while longer to indulge in the excited mood. Then he returned to Erkrather Strasse and watched the transport of the seriously injured Frau

Mantel amidst a crowd of onlookers. There he met the gatekeeper again, who thought he recognized him and asked him where he came from. Kürten was able to fool him with an excuse, then took the dagger from his hiding place and went home. The two seriously injured women could describe the perpetrator, but the description did not lead to the discovery of Kurten. The slightly injured Kornblum had been attacked from behind and had not seen the perpetrator.

On August 24, 1929, Kürten again went out with the dagger in search of victims. At first he was at the main train station unsuccessfully looking for girls. Then he took the tram to Flehe, where a rifle festival was held. He addressed a woman in vain on Aachener Strasse and then watched the fireworks at the shooting festival. He then followed 13-year-old Luise Lenzen and 5-year-old Gertrud Hamacher, who left the marksmen's festival on a dirt road. He spoke to the girls and instructed the older one to get cigarettes for him. When she was out of sight, he choked the 5-year-old who remained with him to the point of unconsciousness, carried her into a bean field and cut her throat there. Then he ran to meet the returning older girl, whom he also choked and dragged into a leek field, where he also put the dagger against her throat. The girl struggled and was able to escape at first, but Kurten soon caught up with her in the field and stabbed her. He left the children's bodies lying there and went home. The bodies were found the next morning.

In the morning after the crime, Kürten returned to the scene of the crime and delighted in the excitement surrounding the place where the bodies were found. He then drove to Oberkassel, where he addressed the 26-year-old domestic worker Gertrud Schulte at the tram stop at Luegplatz, pretended to be a local postal official under a false name, and gained the woman's trust. He persuaded her to visit the fun fair together in Neuss, where they didn't stay too long. On the way back to Oberkassel by tram, he insisted on walking the last stretch. The two got out at Heerdter Rathaus, but instead of the shortest route, Kürten chose a route to the Rheinbogen near Lörick. Schulte, unfamiliar with the place, followed him in good faith to the Rhine meadows, where Kürten sexually assaulted the woman. When she resisted, he stabbed her with the dagger. The tip of the dagger broke off and got stuck in the victim's vertebrae. The woman's cries for help had alarmed several young people nearby. As they approached, Kürten ran away from the scene and threw away the broken dagger. In Leostrasse, he searched the woman's handbag, kept a wristwatch, and threw away the bag and the rest of the contents. He waited for the police to pass by at Lueg Platz and then went home. The victim survived the act seriously injured.

On August 31, 1929, Kürten spoke to Karoline Herstrass, a domestic worker at the main train station in the evening, and with a trick managed to get her to miss the last tram to Neuss. He offered to get her a room and led her to the bank of the Düssel at Ostpark, where he pounced on her. While the woman said that Kürten had thrown her into the river, the police found out that she had jumped on her own initiative and had also inflicted the choke marks on herself. The case remained unresolved.

During this time Kürten regularly visited Maria Hahn's grave. In September 1929, however, he lost interest. He seemed much more interested in the excitement that would be had when Hahn's body was discovered. He therefore made a commented sketch of the grave at the end of September 1929 and threw it into the mailbox of the publishing house of the Düsseldorf city gazette. Nothing is known about the whereabouts of this sketch, nor did the newspaper report about it.

On September 26, 1929, he attacked and gagged Maria Radusch, a domestic worker, in Gerresheim, but the woman escaped him.

On September 29, 1929, Kürten went to Düsseldorf Central Station with a hammer. There he addressed the 31-year-old unmarried domestic worker Ida Reuter. Together they ran over the Rhine bridge to Oberkassel and from there to the Rhine dam, near the place where Kürten had committed the assault on Gertrud Schulte a month earlier. When dusk fell, Reuter insisted on turning back. Kürten agreed, but after a short distance on the way back he suddenly hit the woman with a hammer on the temple. He dragged the unconscious from the Rhine dam down into the less visible Rhine meadows, where he killed her with more hammer blows after dark. He took off the dead woman's trousers and threw them, weighted with pebbles, into the Rhine. Then he took the same way back as after trying to murder Schulte. Again he stopped in Leostraße to search the victim's handbag. This time he kept a ring and threw the rest away. He then returned to the body and began dragging it to the Rhine to sink it into the river. When a man with a dog approached, he abandoned his plans and went home. The man, a police officer on patrol, hadn't noticed. Reuter's body was found early the next morning. During the morning, Kürten returned to the scene of the crime and excitedly watched the police officers working there.

On the evening of October 11, 1929, Kürten went to the center of Düsseldorf with his hammer and looked for victims among cinema-goers between the cinemas on Graf-Adolf-Strasse. There he met 22-year-old Elisabeth Dörrier, who was looking for work and accommodation, with whom he first visited a brewery on Oststrasse before she agreed to come to his apartment. But instead of going to his apartment, he led her to a meadow path on the banks of the Düssel, where he knocked her down on the temple with a hammer blow. He dragged her behind a bush, where he attacked her and injured her with further hammer blows. Assuming she was dead, he left the unconscious woman and threw away her coat, hat, and bag on the way back. The victim was found the following morning and taken to the hospital, but died there after 36 hours without regaining consciousness.

Two days after the crime, he returned to the scene of the crime and met an officer with a sniffer dog, to whom he gave clues about the dead woman's clothes and handbag nearby. However, hel was not suspected. On the same day Kürten made another sketch of the grave of Maria Hahn and this time addressed it to the police administration in Düsseldorf. The sketch was received there the following day, but was too imprecise, so the police initially did not find a body.

On October 25, 1929, Kürten went to Flingern with his hammer in the early evening. There he spoke to a few little girls in vain before meeting 34-year-old Hubertine Meurer in Hellweg. They started talking and walked along Hellweg together. There they also talked about the Scheer murder case, which had happened nearby a few months earlier. When Meurer became suspicious, Kürten hit her on the temple with a hammer blow. He struck another hammer blow on the head of the woman lying on the floor and screaming for help, but then let go of his victim, took her bag and left the scene. At Ostpark, he threw away the victim's bag, which contained only clothing. At Grafenberger Allee he boarded the

JOHN H. DAWSON

tram to Worringerplatz. From there he ran past the main train station to the Hofgarten, where after midnight only a few people stayed. After spending some time in the courtyard garden, he went back along the water to the city. Halfway the prostitute Klara Wanders spoke to him. Kürten was interested, and both went back to the courtyard garden, where Kürten attacked the prostitute at Pineapple Mountain with several hammer blows. The last blow, which left the victim unconscious, broke the hammer handle and the upper part with the hammer head flew into the bushes. Kürten left the victim lying there and moved away in the direction of Hofgartenstrasse. From there he could see that the victim, who had regained consciousness, had started calling for help loudly and was surrounded by several other women at Ratinger Tor. He ran a curve over Jägerhof-Allee back to the Landskrone, got rid of the broken hammer handle there and returned to the scene of the crime, where he unsuccessfully searched for the hammer head.

On November 7, 1929, Kürten again picked up the scissors when he went to Flingern in search of a new victim. At the church in Flingern he met 5-year-old Gertrud Albermann, who played in front of her aunt's house. He persuaded the child to go with him. Kürten also caused no sensation when little Gertrud waved to a family friend as they passed their house. Two mechanics, to whom the man with the child appeared suspicious, speculated whether it

19

was the murderer the police were looking for, but Gertrud's cheerful manner made them believe that it was a father with his daughter. Kürten led the child through the allotment gardens to an allotment area at the Haniel & Lueg factory and choked her there until she passed out. Then he used the scissors to stab her in the temple several times and tried to drink the escaping blood. He then assaulted the child and stabbed her indiscriminately until she was dead. He put the body down in a bush and went home.

The following day, he made a third sketch of Maria Hahn's grave and addressed it to the Düsseldorf newspaper Die Freiheit, which informed the police. This new sketch also contained a reference to the place where he had put Gertrud Albermann's body. Since the letter fell into the hands of the police only a few hours after the body was actually found, the police could assume that only they and the murderer knew about the crime. The letter must therefore have been written by the murderer. Search digs on November 12, 1929 initially did not produce any results. However, after a farmer remembered finding a handbag and keychain nearby during harvest work , Maria Hahn's body was finally recovered on November 15, 1929.

On December 7, 1929, Kürten killed a swan at night in the courtyard garden by cutting his neck. Then he drank the animal's blood.

On February 23, 1930 Kürten met a young domestic

worker, with whom he first visited an inn and then the Grafenberg Forest, where sexual acts occurred in which he choked the woman. When asked about it by the woman, he described the gagging as proof of love. A week later, Kürten met this woman again in his own apartment, but the two were then surprised by Kürten's wife, who had returned earlier.

In March 1930 he lured the ironer Marianne del Santo into the Grafenberg Forest under a pretext, where he began to choke her. The woman managed to escape. A few days later, after a similar incident, he pushed domestic worker Irma Becker down the slope into the Wolfsschlucht in the Grafenberg forest.

On April 13, 1930, he met the domestic worker Gertrud Hau, with whom he went to the courtyard garden after a night at a café, where he harassed her. There was a palpable argument and the woman managed to escape.

On April 30, 1930, he went with the domestic worker Charlotte Ulrich to the Grafenberg Forest, where he struck her with a hammer on the temple and other blows on the head. He initially thought the woman was dead and left, but returned to the scene a few minutes later to make sure. However, the woman had regained consciousness and had fled.

Also in April he made the acquaintance of the young widow Körtzinger, to whom he introduced himself as a bachelor willing to marry. He visited the widow several times in her apartment with the intention of murdering the widow and her children with a hammer or scissors when the opportunity arose. However, the widow had frequent visits from relatives, so that Kürten could no longer act before he was arrested.

On May 14, 1930, Kürten was hanging around Düsseldorf Central Station. He followed the young domestic worker Maria Butlies, who was on her way to the Volksgarten with a harassing man. Kürten spoke to the couple and was able to get the man to leave Butlies alone. He then took the girl to his apartment, where he began making advances. After protests by the woman, Kürten offered to take her to a girls' dormitory in the Grafenberg forest. Once in the forest, he choked the woman, but then let her go and brought her close to a tram stop. Shortly afterwards, Maria Butlies described the incident in a letter to her friend Brückner in Düsseldorf. It was a coincidence that the letter was mistakenly delivered to a Brügmann family on the same street. The family handed it over to the police.

INVESTIGATIONS AND ARRESTS

Investigations into the murders committed by Kürten were unsuccessful for a long time. The then chief prosecutor Otto Steiner awarded Kürten satanic happiness. His well-groomed appearance and friendly manner made him look suspicious, especially when he returned to the crime scenes in public, mingled with the onlookers and sometimes even contacted the investigating officers. At the same time, these qualities had meant that his victims had no suspicion and that even after the first acts became known, he could gain the trust of new victims.

In retrospect, many of the circumstances of the investigation are puzzling. B. the fact that the often police-known Kurten had not been suspected when just a few steps away from his apartment, 9-year-old Rosa Ohliger was murdered. The public relations work of the police in the media was also in its infancy, so neither the evidence found (scissor tip and dagger tip) nor descriptions of the perpetrators of the surviving victims were communicated to the public. It is questionable whether the perpetrator descriptions would ever have resulted in curts, since all witnesses estimated the perpetrator to be between 11 and 24 years younger than he actually was. Ms. Kürten later stated that her husband was putting on make-up to appear younger. However, none of the victims noticed makeup.

The raid and murder series was also not recognized as belonging together for a long time. The reasons are partly that the mentally ill Johann Stausberg indiscriminately confessed to the perpetrator of various murders in Düsseldorf; in addition to three crimes clearly committed by Kürten, also for two further murders according to a different crime pattern, so that some of the crimes were already considered to be solved for a time. Finally, the different crime tools (hammer, scissors, dagger) and the not always available sexual component of the crimes gave reason to believe in different perpetrators. In addition, the police saw in the attacks on Hubertine Meurer and Klara Wanders on October 25, 1929, another perpetrator than in the previous offenses, since the assault on the prostitute Klara Wanders was considered an act of competitive envy in the red light milieu.

Around 12,000 indications of possible perpetrators came from the population. There were at least three references to Kürten. In the course of November 1929, for example, a former inmate of Kürtens reported to the police and stated that he had bragged about similar acts during his time in prison. The police then had photos taken of Kürten to present to the surviving victim Schulte. Ms. Schulte did not recognize the perpetrator in the photos. The police also asked some of Kurten's neighbors about his lifestyle, but they only knew him as a friendly, always well-dressed neighbor.

In view of the unsuccessful outcome of the investigation, unprecedented hysteria spread in Düsseldorf. Under pressure from the media and the public, the Ministry of the Interior set up a special homicide commission and had police forces transferred from Berlin to Düsseldorf. Among them was crime councilor Ernst Gennat, who later recorded his experience in the essay The Düsseldorf Sexual Crimes. He was the first to coined the term serial killer. The series of murders also caused a sensation abroad. The British crime writer Edgar Wallace offered his help to the Düsseldorf criminal police.

The turning point in the investigation only came from Maria Butlies' wrongly delivered letter, in which she reported of her encounter with the perpetrator. The police used Butlies to find the house where the perpetrator was. After a long search, Butlies thought on the morning of May 21, 1930 to recognize the house at 71 Mettmanner Strasse. After Butlies was in the stairwell of the house with a police officer, she was no longer sure whether it was the right house. At noon she returned alone in the hallway of the house, where she told a neighbor about the incidents she had experienced. She also saw Kürten, but did not recognize him. The neighbor wrote Kurten's name on a piece of paper that Butlies handed over to the police in the afternoon. She was now certain that she had recognized the right house, but she had not recognized the perpetrator in the named Kurten.

However, Kürten, who had been unemployed since April 16, had recognized Butlies and had since left the apartment. He withdrew 140 marks from his wife's savings book and met him in the evening in a café, where he told her that he had once again had something with a girl, that he was now on the trail and that he therefore moved out and not the apartment will enter more. There was a scene and Kuerten's wife went home alone while her husband spent the night on the street. The next day he returned to Mettmanner Strasse in the morning, fetched some clothes and then rented a room at Ackerstrasse 53, where he slept throughout the day. In the evening he picked up his wife from work and there was another argument.

The following day, May 23, 1930, the police appeared in the morning at Mettmanner Strasse 71, according to the Butlies, but no one was to be found. The officers then turned to Kürten's wife at her workplace in the Hemesath café and returned to the apartment with her. They informed them about the Butlies robbery and learned that Peter Kürten was unemployed and moved out, but wanted to get his support from the employment office the same day. The officials left a summons for Kürten and went to the job center, where they waited unsuccessfully for the morning.

This police investigation was also unfortunate and was later sharply criticized by government and crime director Willy Gay. You shouldn't have let Butlies return to the house on your own, even if it would have given the decisive clues to Kürten. Gay also criticizes that the police initially only left a subpoena for Kürten, even though he had been among the suspects for some time. The summons were literally an invitation to Kurten to flee.

Kurten had meanwhile returned to Mettmanner Strasse 71 and received the summons from his wife. Confronted with the allegations of an attack on Butlies, he confessed to his wife the act: "Yes, yes, I did everything!" Then Kürten left the apartment again. Around noon he met with his wife on

the popularly known as Sighs Alley, went to an inn with her for lunch and then went with her to the Rhine meadows, where he gave her a two-hour long confession of all the deeds. He rejected his shocked wife's suggestion of committing suicide, if necessary together. Instead, he wanted to leave Düsseldorf and go into hiding. He made an appointment with his wife for a last meeting at Rochuskirche the following afternoon.

In the meantime, Gertrud Schulte, who had been attacked in August 1929, had been presented with further pictures of Kurten, on which she now recognized the perpetrator. Since Kürten was therefore already in question for two acts, the police intensified the search for him and occupied the apartment at Mettmanner Strasse 71, where she arrested the wife of Kürtens, who was returning from the Rhine meadows. When she was interrogated, she first gave the police Kurt's hiding place at Adlerstrasse 53, where he was not. Taken into protective custody because of the risk of darkening, she reported - after she collapsed psychologically - about the planned meeting at the Rochuskirche.

The following day, May 24, 1930, Kürten was arrested at the planned meeting at Rochusmarkt. He made no resistance. Two surviving victims, Gertrud Schulte and Maria Butlies, identified him in a comparison, whereupon Kürten made a comprehensive confession on the same day. In addition to the acts clearly attributable to him, he confessed in his confession to three further murders and four attempted murders in the Altenburg area, which later turned out to be wrong.

Auguste Kürten was very tormented by the "betrayal" of her husband. For this reason, she was temporarily accommodated in the "Grafenberg" mental hospital. She took the wrong name, divorced, and moved to Leipzig after the trial of her former husband.

PRELIMINARY INVESTIGATION, TRIAL AND EXECUTION

During the preliminary investigation, Kürten withdrew his confession in June 1930 and denied all fatalities, but remained committed to confessing to acts in which the victims had survived and also admitted the arson. He justified his earlier admission to his wife by saying that he wanted to help her get the reward for the murderer's arrest.

After juxtaposition with other witnesses and the discovery of hidden objects of the murdered girls and some murder weapons, he returned in August 1930 to an extensive confession of all the deeds. He also revealed the hiding places of four other hammers that he had bought in stock at the end of 1929, praising the properties of these tools, which could cause the victims to lose consciousness with a single blow to the temple.

The preliminary investigation also provided certainty that the letters received with references to the grave sites had clearly been written by Kürten.

One of the tasks of the preliminary examination was the examination of Kuerten's state of mind, for which he was briefed for eight weeks in the Provincial Healing and Nursing Home Bedburg-Hau, where he was examined by the director of the institution Raether and other doctors, who recorded over 1,000 pages of examination reports. The Bedburg institutional doctors as well as other court and institutional doctors consulted unanimously attested that there were no symptoms of the presence of a mental illness in any form. They attested to Kürten a sadistic tendency and full responsibility for his actions.

He owed his nickname "Vampire of Dusseldorf" to his report that he had sucked blood from the wound of a swan chick that he had killed by a neck cut in front of the Parkhotel in Düsseldorf (today the Steigenberger group) in the courtyard garden. According to the filed court and police files, it is certain that he committed similar acts on two, possibly three human victims.

The jury trial against Kürten began on April 13, 1931, under the chair of the district court director Rose. The lawyer Alex Wehner from Düsseldorf acted as defender. The interrogation of Kürten took place in camera, but press representatives were admitted. Kurten repeated his confession before the court. His lawyer asserted the defendant's heavy youth, but also admitted that Kürten had excavated his grave with his actions. In his closing words, Kürten tried to partly blame his victims for making it "very easy" for him, but also confessed that he could not escape the death penalty and asked the relatives of the victims to forgive them.

The Düsseldorf jury sentenced him to death nine times on 22 April 1931 for murder in nine cases, as well as 15 years in prison for the seven attempted murders. An alleged killing of two boys on the banks of the Rhine in Mülheim in 1893, to which Kürten had also pleaded, was disregarded in the judgment due to the lack of detection and criminal responsibility.

While Kürten had visibly enjoyed the preliminary investigation and the trial, as there was a great interest in him and he was granted various benefits and special requests during pre-trial detention, he was visibly dissatisfied after the verdict was pronounced. He was a normal prisoner and no one paid any attention to him. He then had his lawyer submit a petition for mercy.

The spectacular case and the verdict passed sparked a vocal discussion in the press and the public, which soon went far beyond the Kürten case and dealt with general questions about the death penalty.

The Prussian government rejected Kurten's request for mercy on June 30. On July 1, Kürten was transferred to the Klingelpütz prison in Cologne. There he was informed in the afternoon of the rejection of the request for mercy and the execution scheduled for the following morning. Kürten asked for spiritual assistance, whereupon the pastor was put at his side and his confessor arrived in Cologne in the evening. He spent the night sleepless in the company of the clergy and his lawyer, and wrote letters to his wife, surviving victims of his deeds, and surviving dependents. At 5 a.m. he attended another mass he had read before he was executed at 6 a.m. by executioner Carl Gröpler with the guillotine.

Despite all secrecy, a group of reporters gathered in front of the Klingelpütz before the execution. They were denied access to the execution, but a judicial spokesman informed them of the decision. The execution of Kurten was unanimously positive in the press.

Kuerten's body was handed over to some doctors present to examine and take specimens. Among other things, the scientists also examined the brain for abnormal changes. The body was buried without a head. The mummified head came to the United States after World War II and is now an exhibit in the Ripley's Believe It or Not! to visit in Wisconsin Dells.

ARTISTIC
RECEPTION

Literature

Stephen King refers to Kürten in his novel Salem must Burn. In 2007 Alisha Bionda and Jörg Kleudgen placed the figure Peter Kürten in the novel The Vampire of Düsseldorf, Volume 9 of the series Wolfgang Hohlbein's Shadow Chronicle, in a correspondingly vampiric frame. The crime novel published by Jo Nesbø Durst in 2017 also makes reference to Kürten.

JOHN H. DAWSON

Film and theater

Fritz Lang's film M is based in part on the case.

In 1964 Robert Hossein made the film The Man Who Was Peter Kürten (Le Vampire de Düsseldorf) with himself in the title role in France.

The story of Peter Kürten is also the subject of Anthony Neilson's play Normal - The Düsseldorf Ripper, which premiered in 1991. It deals with the idea that a murderer is slumbering in every person.

In the 1995 plot of the US feature film Copykill, references to the Kürten case are also made.

Slaughter Festival or How to become a useful victim, a play by Thomas Richhardt about Peter Kürten and his wife Auguste, was premiered in July 2000 at the Düsseldorfer Schauspielhaus.

In September 2008 the Kammerspiel Who is the Murderer? premiered by WA Wirringa at the Düsseldorf Altstadtherbst. The text was taken from historical minutes and condensed dramaturgically.

The Czech-Macedonian film Normal - The Düsseldorf Ripper dates from 2009 and is also based on the story of Peter Kürten and the play of the same name.

The case is also named in the series Blood Gang of the RTL series The Clever. In this episode, a grandson of Kürtens commits murders and assault in the same order and order as his grandfather.

Music

The American songwriter Randy Newman, whose first wife Roswitha comes from Düsseldorf, published the song In Germany Before the War in 1977 on his album Little Criminals, the text of which refers to Peter Kürten and one of the acts from the perspective of the child murderer describes:

"A little girl has lost her way, with hair of gold and eyes of gray ... We lie beneath the autumn sky, my little golden girl and I. And she lies very still."

The British power electronics band Whitehouse dedicated Peter Kürten released the 1981 album Dedicated To Peter Kurten Sadist And Mass Slayer. The American metal band Macabre dedicated a song to the serial killer entitled The Vampire of Düsseldorf. The Canadian metal band Dahmer released the song Peter Kürten on a split with the band Denak in 1997.

In 1999 the French black metal band Namtar released a song on their demo tape entitled The Düsseldorf Vampire, which deals with this topic.

The album Set Sail to Mystery by the Gothic metal band The Vision Bleak, released in April 2010, contains the song I Dined with the Swans, which refers to Peter Kürten's act of drinking swan blood. The singer of the depressive black metal band Shining, Niklas Kvarforth, sang an alternative version of the song for the 2-CD special edition.

The Japanese doom metal band Church of Misery refers twice to Kürten on their 2013 album Thy

JOHN H. DAWSON

Kingdom Scum. On the one hand, the front cover consists of an edited police photo from Kürtens, on the other hand, the more than twelve-minute, psychedelic piece Dusseldorf Monster (Peter Kurten) deals with his deeds.

May his victims rest in peace.

37